IT DOESN'T WORK HERE
THE EVOLUTION OF THE BUSINESS LEADERSHIP CONCEPT
AND ITS APPLICABILITY TO DEVELOPING MARKETS

ALI DERISAVI

*To my family and
all the good people of the world.*

CONTENTS

> *If, occasionally, historical evidence does not square with formulated laws, it should be remembered that a law is but a deduction from experience and experiment, and therefore laws must conform with historical facts, not facts with laws.*
>
> Immanuel Velikovsky, *Worlds in Collision*

PREFACE

When I received my first C at the beginning of my MBA program, I felt like it was the end of the world. Being an A student and graduating with distinction made any grade but an A unthinkable to me. But it took me a long time to discover that in a purely scientific environment a problem cannot have more than one correct answer—you can be either right or wrong. But when it comes to the different disciplines of art, one can find more than one correct answer to the same problem.

The dilemma is that some people, especially those in the world of academia, have been trying to turn art into science and apply the laws that were deduced from their experiences to totally different facts.

As a student, arguing against or challenging this matter would leave you with Cs, Ds and sometines Fs. Hence, to pass one would be left with no choice but to become a hypocrite and tell them whatever they want to hear.

This disease has unfortunately spread beyond the academy into more powerful circles.
Globalization, driven by world powers, is imposing new rules and laws on the world regardless of the facts of the developing societies. And for the recipients of these new laws, it is no longer a matter of grades; it is a matter of life and death. Trying to challenge the laws of globalization and the new world order is equivalent to committing suicide.

This humble work is the result of more than a decade of observation, reading, thinking, listening, and talking about the related subjects. In writing this book, my aim was to shed light on the European cultural and socioeconomic evolution that followed the Renaissance and to describe the cultural differences between the West and the rest of the world. I argue that systems such as democracy and capitalism are the fruits of more than 600 years of intellectual, religious, political, and social evolution and that imposing them on societies that have developed along totally different lines results in nothing but chaos, or, to be politically correct, "creative" chaos.

The business leadership concept, a by-product of this cultural evolution, serves as a prime example to show why most modern western business principles are inapplicable in the rest of the world.

Many of those who read the draft of this manuscript found it too short and suggested that it could benefit from more examples and case studies. Indeed, every title referenced here could be a subject of multiple books, but a deeper examination of related subjects means more time. While writing in this part of the world has unfortunately not yet become a profession that can provide a sustainable living for more than a few, one has no choice but to spend most of his or her time in more financially rewarding endeavors. Certainly, not all the arguments raised in the book are exhaustively addressed, but it is to be hoped that after reading it, readers will develop an interest in further analysis of its related subjects.

In the conclusion of the book, I offer my personal understanding of how one is to tackle the issue of development in the developing societies. My recommendations, while abstract, could, I believe, serve as a starting point for the long journey toward true development. God willing.

ACKNOWLEDGEMENTS

This book is the product of more than ten years of interaction with people. I am deeply indebted to those who talked, listened, argued, agreed and disagreed with me; they have certainly taught me much of what I think I know today. I am very grateful for their direct and indirect contribution to the creation of this humble work.

Prior to publishing, I distributed copies of the draft of this manuscript and received constructive feedback that helped me enhance the final product. I am deeply grateful to my wife Virginia for her continuous support and to Ahmad Naseri, Ali Kanaan, Dana Swoidan, Maureen McFillin, Rabea Hajjar, Rashdia Baiwala, and Richard Bushman for their valuable comments and criticism.

I would like to particularly thank Mr. Riadh Al Hassani for his valuable insights and his suggestion that I turn some of the book's ideas into illustrations.

I am also grateful to Mr. Abdul Aziz Dandashi for his help in producing the illustrations.

I also thank Mr. Bill Gibson for helping me select the title of this book.

INTRODUCTION

In the early 1990s, while I was still a college student, I noticed a questionnaire in the local newspaper that claimed that answering its questions would identify how good a leader one could be. That was my first encounter with the concept of leadership. It was also the time when I started to develop a desire to learn more about the subject. *What is leadership? How does it relate to business? And why is it a relatively new concept compared, for example, to the concept of management?* These were among the first questions I had to seek the answers to. Obviously, questions such as, *What are the traits of a leader?* and *Are leaders born or made?* and assessing the difference between leadership and management, were also key questions that had to be addressed. However, they were secondary compared to the earlier ones. It was the "why" that drew my attention rather than the "how."

Throughout my research on the subject, I encountered various theories, definitions, and styles of leadership and found that the personality traits of a leader were noticeably the most cultivated subject. However, in most of the leadership literature, a fundamental (and parallel) set of issues was hardly addressed: Why do we need leadership? Why isn't the "command and control" style of management considered appropriate anymore? Why should we start to consider emotions in the modern business environment? Why do we have to stop ordering and start asking? What changed the business environment?

In the pursuit of answers to these questions, I was faced with yet deeper and more interesting issues. I discovered that the forces that brought change to the business environment were not exclusive to it. The gradual transformation of land ownership and governance in medieval European feudal societies, the rise of the bourgeoisie, and the emergence of modern (and contemporary) capitalist societies were all part of a millennial cultural evolution that had its roots in the dawn of the European Renaissance and its flowering in the Enlightenment of the 18th century and the Industrial Revolution of the 19th century. What initiated this cultural movement is a question open for debate and is beyond the scope of this book. One thing, however, is clear: this cultural evolution introduced many new concepts, chief among them the concept of human rights. The birth of the concept of the rightful treatment of all men marked a new era in human history and mandated a new set of rules with which to govern his (and more recently, also her) economic, political, and social affairs. The work environment was not an exception; it had to adapt and cater to the needs of the modern worker. From then on, business theorists realized that the long-standing command and control style of business management was dying away and that new theories of governance would have to be developed to deal with the modern rights-oriented employee. Thus, the old master–slave relationship gradually transformed into the contemporary leader–follower form.

Certainly a thorough understanding of the reasons behind the development of the concept of business leadership was of great value in the process of applying it in a developing environment.

Three years into my career, when I had been promoted to a managerial position, my superior sarcastically told me, "so far you have been a unionist, now you are a manager. So you have to look at things, think, and act differently." His comments dragged us into a serious argument about democracy, human rights, motivation, and increased productivity. I was eager to convince him that the application of these new egalitarian concepts would surely yield better results. But his conversation stopper was, "It doesn't work here!"

I left his office determined to prove him wrong, but eleven years down the road, I am thinking that maybe he had a point!

DEFINING LEADERSHIP

There probably are as many definitions for leadership as there are leaders, books, and academic papers on the subject.

"The research on leadership has produced many definitions of the term." (Kreitner, 1995, p. 469)

Moreover, Jack Welch (2005, p. 62) argues that, if asked, each leader would give a different list of leadership rules. One common notion, however, in most leadership literature, is the emphasis on the capacity to achieve results. Daniel Goleman, in his *Harvard Business Review* article, "Leadership that Gets Results" (2000, p. 78), stresses this point and states,

"ask any group of businesspeople the question 'What do effective leaders do?' and you'll hear a sweep of answers. Lead-

ers set strategy; they motivate; they create a mission; they build a culture. Then ask 'What should leaders do?' If the group is seasoned you'll likely hear one response: the leader's singular job is to get results."

Accordingly, might one simply define leadership as having the capacity to achieve results? Perhaps, but this would be a very general—and at the same time, somewhat negligent—definition of leadership. It overlooks fundamental questions such as *How are results achieved?* and *Should all achievers be considered leaders?*

Most contemporary leadership literature consider Winston Churchill, Gandhi, Martin Luther King, Nelson Mandela, Richard Branson, Bill Gates, and Steve Jobs to be leaders, simply because they are all achievers. Nevertheless, there is a fundamental difference between Gandhi, Martin Luther King, and Mandela on the one hand and Churchill, Gates, Jobs, and Branson on the other.
Churchill possessed all the formal power and authority associated with a prime minister's position. Branson, Gates, and Jobs have the power to hire, fire, and promote and demote employees.

But what kind of authority did Gandhi, King, and Mandela have? They mobilized millions of people and achieved great results—but without any formal authority.

Thus, mere accomplishment of results is not the sole measure by which to identify leadership qualities. The ability to influence people without formal authority is the fundamental ingredient of true leadership.

In the business context, leadership is defined as

> "a social influence process in which the leader seeks the voluntary participation of subordinates in an effort to reach organizational objectives." (Kreitner, 1995, p. 469)

In the same book, Kreitner defines management as

> "the process of working with and through others to achieve organizational objectives in a changing environment." (Kreitner, p. 4)

According to these definitions, both leaders and managers seek to achieve organizational objectives. However, it should be noted that unlike managers, leaders ought to accomplish their goals through the voluntary participation of subordinates. The word "voluntary" used in the leadership definition indicates free will and choice. Participants can simply choose not to volunteer! The absence of the word "voluntary" in the definition of management indicates that participants are legally obliged to follow the manager. This in turn entitles the manager of legitimate power to impose demands on the participants. We can therefore conclude that leadership could be defined as "achieving results without authority" in comparison to management, where results are achieved through the exercise of formal authority.

While most business literature does not draw a line between these roles and uses the terms interchangeably, understanding the difference between them is of vital importance in their application within the business environment. Drawing a line between leadership as a position and leadership as a skill would also help clarify that those so-called leaders at the top of an organization's pyramid might not necessarily have what it takes to be a leader.

Through their formal authority, business executives might enforce the participation of their subordinates; however, the participation of peers, superiors, customers, and suppliers can only be accomplished by mastering the primary leadership skill: the art and science of influencing people without the exercise of authority. Allan Cohen and David Bradford, in their book *Influence without Authority* (2005, p. 3), argue that

> *"you need to influence those in other departments and divisions, that is, people you can't order and control. You need to influence your manager and others above*

you and you certainly can't order and control them!"

This leads us to the fundamental question of how to influence others without the use of authority. Kreitner (1995, p. 469) suggests that

"to encourage voluntary participation, leaders supplement any authority and power they possess with their personal attributes and social skills."

Thus, according to Kreitner, personal attributes and social skills are the key qualities a leader should possess in order to influence people without resorting to (or having access to) authority. Although the terms "personal attributes" and "social skills" might sound very familiar to most of us, and their value in influencing people might fall under the category of common sense, the lack of a deep understanding of these notions and their related human psychology would leave most leaders with a narrow set of tactics that would only yield short-term results.

James Clawson, in his article "A Leader's Guide to Why People Behave the Way They Do" (2001, p. 2) argues that

"ignorance of the fundamentals of human behavior leaves one with a limited set of generic influence models that may or may not have impact on any particular individ-

ual. Deeper understanding provides more options, gives one more potential tools, and frankly, makes one a more powerful leader."

A Machiavelian and superficial approach to using influencing models might yield results in the short term but would certainly not be able to sustain more substantial results. In his book *The 7 Habits of Highly Effective People* (1990, p. 21) Stephen Covey argues that

> *"if I try to use human influence strategies and tactics of how to get other people to do what I want, to work better, to be more motivated, to like me and each other – while my character is fundamentally flawed, marked by duplicity and insincerity – then, in the long run, I cannot be successful. My duplicity will breed distrust, and everything I do – even using so-called good human relations techniques – will be perceived as manipulative."*

It has been argued that a good understanding of people's needs and what they really value is a key element in the process of influencing them. Cohen and Bradford (2005, p. 16):

> *"There are numerous ways of categorizing influence behavior. You can influence people by methods such as rational persuasion, inspirational appeal, consultation,*

ingratiation, personal appeal, forming a coalition, or relentless pressure. Although it is tempting to think of each of these methods as a separate tactic, we believe that exchange – trading something valued for what you want – is actually the basis for all of them."

The authors add (p. 17) that

"none of these tactics succeeds, however, if the receiver does not perceive benefit of some kind, a payment in a valued currency."

Thus, it is extremely important for leaders to learn about the currency that those who they want to influence, value the most. In the Harvard Business School Press article "Influence: Your Mechanism for Using Power" (2005, p. 10), the author, commenting on Cohen and Bradford's metaphor of currencies of exchange, asserts that

"the key to using currencies effectively is to understand what other people want and value. You gain that understanding when you move beyond a superficial level of knowing what motivates, inspires, and concerns people. What really matters to them? What threatens them or stands in the way of their success? How does their view of the world and the organization differ from yours? If you answer these deeper

questions, you will be much better posi-
tioned to make exchanges and influence
the people with whom you do business."

This is, however, more easily said than done. Moving beyond a superficial level of human-influence tactics requires a reasonable level of knowledge of human psychology and the social sciences. This is not to suggest that a leader should be a professional psychologist, but awareness of concepts such as perception, emotions, motivation, personality traits, and the qualities of interpersonal relationships would certainly leave a leader in a better position to identify needs and seek ways to satisfy them.

While needs may differ depending on the various aspects of cultures, groups, organizations, and individuals, there are many theories that could assist leaders to identify needs. It is safe to say that Abraham Maslow's theory of the hierarchy of needs is probably the most well known.

Maslow separated the needs of every human being into five categories: physiological, safety, social, esteem, and self-actualization. He then further separated them into higher and lower order. Physiological and safety needs are categorized as lower-order needs and social, esteem, and self-actualization are categorized as higher-order needs. Maslow believed that a substantial satisfaction of a lower-order need leads to the domination of a higher-order need.

Similarly, Freud's structural theory divides the self into the hierarchical elements of id, ego, and superego, wherein the id represents unmediated pleasure, superego the sense of morals (or society), and the ego the conscious self (the mind), doer of either or both the promptings of the id or the superego. One's prevailing needs are totally dependent on the shifting dominance of one of these divisions of the self.

Learning about Gandhi, Martin Luther King, and Mandela—true leaders that mobilized millions without authority—makes us wonder about the nature of the needs they identified and the values they delivered.

> *"I have cherished the ideal of a democratic and free society in which all persons live together in harmony with equal opportunities."* (Benjamin Pogrund quoting Mandela, 2003, p. 5)

Gandhi, Mandela, and others like them promised freedom, independence, and sometimes salvation. These intangible notions certainly do not fall under the category of lower-level needs. A study of the experiences of great leaders, those who influenced millions of people without possessing any formal authority, suggests that not only were they able to deliver higher-level values to satisfy higher-level needs, they were also successful in educating and transcending their followers to discover their higher-level desires for themselves. Clawson (2001) argues that the ability to consciously transcend our inherited ideas and beliefs and become more aware is the mark of visionary leadership.

"I have not the shadow of a doubt that any man or woman can achieve what I have, if he or she would make the same effort and cultivate the same hope and faith." (Michael Nicholson quoting Gandhi, 2003, p. 23)

In the context of business, these leaders are labeled as level 5, emotionally intelligent, inspirational, charismatic, informal, and/or transformational. Regardless of the name, such leaders are individuals who identify and deliver noble values that satisfy higher-level human needs. They influence followers and achieve results without possession of or reliance on formal authority. Their trading currency, or the value they provide in exchange for the support they receive from followers, could not be calculated using ordinary units of measurement.

Ideas and values such as trust, love, honesty, transparency, courage, achievement, recognition, growth, independence, and freedom are among the non-measurable, non-materialistic but essential currencies those leaders must convey.

Although drawing a line between leadership and management creates a better understanding and application of both concepts, it should not be implied that the two concepts are opposing approaches that cannot be exercised in parallel. To succeed in the modern business environment, one has to master both skills.

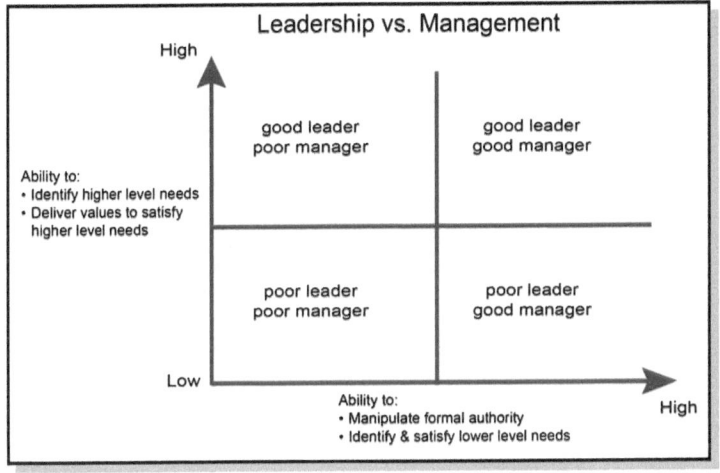

> *The fundamental rights of [humanity] are, first: the right of habitation; second, the right to move freely; third, the right to the soil and subsoil, and to the use of it; fourth, the right of freedom of labor and of exchange; fifth, the right to justice; sixth, the right to live within a natural national organization; and seventh, the right to education.*
>
> *Albert Schweitzer*

THE EVOLUTION OF THE BUSINESS LEADERSHIP CONCEPT

Leadership, defined earlier as the ability to influence people without the use of authority, is not a new concept. Human history is primarily about great leaders. However, the introduction of the leadership concept in the business environment is a relatively new phenomenon.

Most contemporary leadership theories directly link successful leadership with the ability to manage one's own emotions and those of others, an ability that is sometimes referred to as emotional intelligence. Daniel Goleman, the author of *Emotional Intelligence* (1995), identifies six styles of leadership and links each one of them to a different component of emotional intelligence. He claims that the effectiveness of the leadership concept is entirely dependent on how we employ emotions. However, it is also well known that there was very little room in the business environment for emotions until recently.

> "Since the late nineteenth century and the rise of scientific management, organizations have been specifically designed with the objective of trying to control emotions. A well-run organization was one that successfully eliminated frustration, fear, anger, love, hate, joy, grief and similar feelings. Such emotions were the antithesis of rationality. So, although researchers and managers knew that emotions were an inseparable part of everyday life, they tried to create organizations that were emotion-free." (Stephen Robbins, *Organizational Behavior*, 2005, p. 113)

Realizing that successful leadership is entirely reliant on the proper treatment of emotions but that well-run organizations of the late nineteenth century were emotion-free, we can easily conclude that the business leadership concept did not exist at least until then. Goleman (2000, p. 80) further elaborates that *"it has been more than a decade since research first linked aspects of emotional intelligence to business results."*

So why was leadership theory introduced into the world of business? Do we really need to consider emotions in the work environment and consequently require leaders to address issues of emotions? Why all of a sudden has leadership become a prerequisite for running successful business organizations? Why doesn't the command and control style of management work anymore? Is leadership a real necessity, or is it an artificial need created and marketed by training consultants?

To answer these questions, one cannot isolate the business leadership concept from its surrounding environment. Business leadership is only a by-product of a greater cultural evolution that gradually changed the behavior of the modern man toward authority. In his *Harvard Business Review* article "Managing Oneself," Peter Drucker (1999, p. 70) states that

> *"throughout history, the great majority of people never had to ask the question, What should I contribute? They were told what to contribute, and their tasks were dictated either by the work itself – as it was for the peasant or artisan – or by a master or a mistress, as it was for domestic servants. And until very recently, it was taken for granted that most people were subordinates who did as they were told. Even in*

the 1950s and 1960s, the new knowledge workers (the so-called organization men) looked to their company's personnel department to plan their careers. Then in the late 1960s, no one wanted to be told what to do any longer. Young men and women began to ask, What do I want to do?"

Choosing not to be told what to do and deciding to do what one wants to do indicates a shift in attitude, a shift not exclusive to the business environment. The business environment was only a part of the bigger picture. The emergence of democratic society was a greater outcome of that attitude shift, which was neither coincidental nor a product of a sudden revolution. It has been argued that the emergence of the concept of human rights in medieval Europe laid the foundation for profound social, political, and economic changes which, through the course of centuries, resulted in the birth of the contemporary rightful man—one who does not want to be told what to do.

Micheline Ishay, author of *The History of Human Rights from Ancient Times to the Globalization Era* (2004), presents a history of this attitude shift. She states (p. 64) that

> *"the next three centuries [following the sixteenth century], however, were to witness a revolutionary change in human thoughts as for the first time a secular and relatively more egalitarian approach to universal*

morality emerged in Europe and spread throughout the world under the revolutionary banner of the Enlightenment."

Although a few scholars argue that the concept of human rights existed in most ancient cultures, most historians believe that much of modern human rights law, and its universal nature, is a product of medieval Europe. Ishay believes that the European Enlightenment, the creation of wealth, the Industrial Revolution, the emergence of the middle class, and the socialist movement of the nineteenth century all played a major role in the birth of the modern human rights movement.

"If the civilizations and ethical contributions of China, India and the Muslim world towered over those of medieval Europe, it is equally true that the legacy of the European Enlightenment, for our current understanding of human rights, supersedes other influences. The necessary conditions for the Enlightenment, which combined to bring an end to the Middle Ages in Europe, included the scientific revolution, the rise of mercantilism, the launching of maritime explorations of the globe, the consolidation of nation-states, and the emergence of the middle class. These developments stimulated the expansion of Western power even as they created propitious prospects for the development of modern conceptions of human rights. They ultimately shat-

*tered feudalism and challenged the pre-
viously uncontested divine rights of kings."*
(Ishay, p. 7)

In her book, Ishay sheds light on more details of
the development of the concept of human rights;
nevertheless, a careful analysis of the interrelated
concepts introduced in the above paragraph
would sufficiently serve the purpose of this argument. It is argued that the creation of wealth due
to maritime exploration and trade helped speed
the emergence of the new middle class. This new
social class, empowered by its access to education, ownership of capital, and financial independence from the state and the nobility demanded
far more civil and political rights. Members of this
new social class challenged not only the authority
of its kings, but all kinds of authority, including the
authority of God and the church.

Galileo Galilei's conflict with the church is a well-
known example of a challenge to the highest
authorities of early modern times. Observably,
over time, the struggle for rights and the resulting
confrontation with authority intensified and even
turned violent. The 1776 Virginia Declaration of
Rights, the 1789 French Declaration of the Rights
of Man and of the Citizen and the Universal Declaration of Human Rights of 1948 were the more
noticeable products of vicious wars for freedom
and equality. The evolution and maturity of the
concept of human rights led, by the nineteenth
century, to profound transformation in western so-

cieties and all their entities. The work environment was not an exception; it, too, had to adapt to the demands of modern man. On the effect of this concept on the work environment Ishay (p. 9) explains that

> "*the nineteenth-century industrial revolution and the growth of the labor movement opened the gates of freedom to previously marginalized individuals who challenged the classical liberal economic conception of social justice.*" She continues, "*From the nineteenth century onwards, radical and reformist socialists alike called for redefining the liberal agenda to include increased economic equity, the right to organize trade unions, child welfare, universal suffrage, restriction of the workday, the right to education, and other social welfare rights.*"

Obviously, the master–servant or lord–vassal relationship that governed the work environment of feudal Europe did not include the demands and expectations of the modern rights-oriented employee.

One of the most important products of this sustained quest for human rights was the right to organize a trade union, an entity with the primary objective of protecting workers' rights. The formation of trade unions created a new situation for employers. They had to deal with a more powerful workforce that demanded better wages, better work conditions and rules, and policies to govern their work environments. Kreitner (1995, p. 50) describing the rise of organized labor, states that

> *"to understand why the human relations movement evolved, one needs first to appreciate its sociopolitical background. From the late 1800s to the 1920s, American industry grew by leaps and bounds as it attempted to satisfy the many demands of a rapidly growing population. Cheap immigrant labor was readily available, and there was a seller's market for finished goods. Then came the Great Depression in the 1930s, and millions stood in bread lines instead of pay lines. Many held business somehow responsible for the depression, and public sympathy swung from management to labor. Congress consequently began to pass prolabor legislation. When the Wagner Act of 1935 legalized union-management collective bargaining, management began searching for ways to stem the tide of all-out unionization. Early human relation theory proposed an enticing answer: satisfied employees would be less inclined to join unions. Business managers subsequently began adopting morale-boosting human relations techniques as a union-avoidance tactic."*

It is notable that what we know as business leadership today can be described as a "union-avoidance tactic" in the early twentieth century. It is certain that the introduction of the concept into the business environment was due to an environmental shift that resulted in the inability of business managers to continue to exercise the long-standing command and control style of management.

Similarly, Bruner et al, in their book *The Portable MBA* (2003) argue that the "liberalization of markets" and "liberalization of political institutions in society" are the changes that profoundly affected business environment and caused the shift away from the command and control style of management to a more humanitarian style of corporate governance.

Undoubtedly, liberalization, the development of the concept of human rights, and the birth of the rights-invested man, diminished the authority of the business managers. In today's western work environment, managers have to manage with less (or sometimes no) authority and employees need to be motivated, not commanded, to achieve results.

Certainly, the concept of human rights will develop even further and so will the concept of business leadership. It could be that our current system of corporate governance will be labeled "modern slavery" a hundred years from now.

"Shout, and people will fear you."

Proverb

THE APPLICABILITY OF THE BUSINESS LEADERSHIP CONCEPT TO THE DEVELOPING MARKETS

Some scholars believe that contemporary western democratic society, capitalism, secularism, and socialism are all products of the concept of human rights. Others identify capital and the ability to create wealth as the root cause of the development of the human-rights concept. This is certainly a great and ongoing debate; however, one thing is evident: regardless of which came first or which is primary, all these forces are interrelated and co-dependent. Their co-dependency suggests that one cannot survive without the others. A thorough examination of European cultural evolution after the Enlightenment confirms that these ideas, in their contemporary form, developed in an interrelated and parallel manner. Historical evidence confirms that attempts to introduce one of theses social sub-systems into a society that lacks the others almost always disturbs the social equilibrium.

Hernando De Soto, in his book *The Mystery of Capital: Why Capitalism Triumphs in the West and Fails Everywhere Else* (2000), gives notable examples of how the introduction of capitalism into some less developed markets disturbed the status quo:

> *"In the last decade, ever since both regions [Latin America and Russia] began to build capitalism without capital, they have shared the same political, social, and economic problems: glaring inequality, underground economies, pervasive mafias, political instability, capital flight, flagrant disregard for the law."* (p. 9)

Introducing capitalism into socially hindered societies or introducing democracy into backward economies was doomed to failure and for the most part yielded ugly consequences. These failures give evidence that although these ideas might survive for a while, they definitely cannot be sustained over a long period of time.

George Soros, while a defender of global capitalism, says in his book, *George Soros on Globalization* (2002), that introducing capitalism into less-developed societies has created some distortions. One of the most dramatic setbacks of globalization, according to Soros, is the "penetration of market values into areas where they do not properly belong." He correctly states that newly introduced market values are not in harmony with other social values of the less-developed societies. Soros further argues that one way for these societies to benefit from capitalism would be implementation of political and institutional reforms leading to an "Open Society." Soros's conclusion is correct. Introducing an out-of-the-ordinary social sub-system into a traditional society would disturb the status quo. Social sub-systems should develop in parallel. However, it is a fact that social development is a gradual process and does not happen over-night.

De Soto (2000), explaining the inability of the less-developed countries to benefit from capitalism, argues that they missed lessons from US history. He states that

> "Americans and Europeans have been telling the other countries of the world, 'You have to be more like us.' In fact, they are very much like the United States of a century ago when it too was an undeveloped country," (p. 9)

If, as De Soto claims, it took the Americans a hundred years to integrate capitalism and its values into their society, there is no reason to believe that other countries could do the same thing over-night. Moreover, it should be understood that western social evolution was the result of an amalgamation of social, political, and cultural forces over a long period of time. History tells us that conscious engineering of social development usually does not produce the desired results. Abdol Karim Soroush, the distinguished Iranian philosopher, in his book *Reason, Freedom, and Democracy in Islam* (2000), presents a lucid distinction between the West's and the developing world's socioeconomic experiences. He states that

> "historians and sociologists agree that the values that preceded, caused, and sustained the development of the west were not the result of a conscious world-historical project of their authors. Bacon, Luther, and Machiavelli did not set out to create the contemporary civilization of the west, nor were they aware of their crucial role as the architects of a monumental change in the history of the world. Yet, the empirical science of Bacon, the secular religion of Luther, and the amoral politics of Machiavelli combined with other relevant ideas and events to create the edifice of the modern world. The dilemma of the developing nations is that they want to engineer this change consciously. Thus they missed important historical opportunities because they provoked forms of resistance that did not inhibit the west." (p. 41)

Soros's vision of transforming the less-developed societies into open societies as a prerequisite for adopting capitalism might be theoretically a viable proposal. But conscious implementation of this theory, according to Soroush, would not yield the desired results.

Karl Popper, in his book *The Open Society and Its Enemies* (1945) defines an open society as a democratic society in which political leaders are overthrown peacefully rather than through revolutions and coups d'etat. Attempts to transform less-developed, mostly autocratic (or totalitarian) societies into open democratic societies in an effort to introduce free-market values have frequently produced shocking and unpredicted consequences. Amy Chua in her book, *World on Fire: How Exporting Free Market Democracy Breeds Ethnic Hatred and Global Instability* (2003), argues that introducing "overnight democracy" into less-developed societies would almost always result in a negative social reaction. Chua states that

> *"it is striking to note that at no point of history did any Western nation ever implement laissez-faire capitalism and overnight universal suffrage at the same time – the precise formula of free market democracy currently being pressed on developing countries around the world."* (p. 14)

Taking Iraq as an example, Chua further explains how a hasty attempt to turn Iraq into a liberal, western-style free-market democracy created nothing but chaos.

Iraq represents a recent (and striking) example of chaos brought about by introducing western market values into a culture where they do not properly belong. Less significant chaotic cases are frequently observed when western and western-oriented businesses attempt to introduce some of their principles into less-developed markets.

In their book *The 86 Percent Solution: How to Succeed in the Biggest Market Opportunity of the 21st Century* (2006), Vijay Mahajan and Kamini Banga describe the status of the market in the developing societies:

> *"Customers in these markets also have not yet developed a culture of consumerism. They don't know how to be customers, so strategies used in the developed markets, such as money-back guarantees, can have unexpected effects."* (p. 19)

The authors share some very interesting stories of how introducing western concepts into the developing markets have had unpredictable results:

> *"In most developed markets, Amway uses a no-questions-asked money-back guarantee to signal product quality...This guarantee showed that the company stood behind its products unconditionally. When Amway offered the same guarantee in China in 1997, it ran into trouble. Customers began returning empty bottles for refunds*

after using the product. A barbershop found that it could use Amway shampoo for free returning every empty bottle for a full refund. Then enterprising third parties began repackaging the soap and returning the empty bottles right away. Unemployed Shanghai residents paid $84 for an initial set of products as an Amway distributor and never ran out. Others just scrounged empty bottles from trashcans and turned them in for refunds. One enterprising collector received nearly $10,000 for sacks full of old bottles. When refunds mounted to $100,000 per day, Amway realized something was fundamentally wrong." (p. 41)

As argued earlier, the concept of business leadership is a by–product of western free-market democracy. If, according to Chua, bringing democracy to a less-developed society will result in backlash, there is no reason to believe that bringing democracy or any of its extensions to the society's business environment will not also result in backlash. After all, members of the less-developed societies and their business environments are one and the same!

Throughout my teaching experience, 70 percent of business executives (mostly from developing markets) believe that Douglas McGregor's "theory X" (in *The Human Side of Enterprise*, 1960) is a better way to govern people than "theory Y." Under theory X, McGregor argues, employees inherently dislike work and responsibility and must be forced and threatened to achieve results. Theory Y is exactly the opposite. We can assume, then, that the command and control style of management is still the preferred and applicable approach of governing people in the developing societies.

In his speech on democracy at a conference held at the Emirates International Forum in Dubai, Marathir Mohammad, the former prime minister and architect of modern Malaysia, stated that

> "we really don't understand how it works, especially liberal democracy, and it will do us more damage than whatever system we practice in our countries. It is not the system that matters. It is good governance by good people that we need."

He continued:

> "Feudal kings, even dictators, have provided and can provide good governance."

I share this point of view; the dilemma, however, is that not all the kings and dictators of the developing markets are able to provide good governance. Thus, if change and development are to be brought to these societies, the responsibility for bringing them in will have to fall on other people's shoulders.

> *You can accomplish anything in life, provided that you do not mind who gets the credit.*
>
> *Harry Truman*

LEADING FROM THE MIDDLE

A quick examination of the current governing systems of most developing countries reveals that they are far from being open societies. Some of them have been ruled by the same ruler or ruling party for decades, and change usually comes either through coups d'etat or the death of a ruler—but never through democratic means. In an interview with Al Jazeera TV, Amine Gemayel, the former president of Lebanon, sarcastically told the interviewer that he was lucky to be able to talk to a former president in the Arab world because in the Arab world usually you can only find "late presidents"!

It has been argued that the main reason why the developing countries are always developing but never developed is their corrupt governments. Soros (2002) argues that next to armed conflicts, oppressive and corrupt regimes and weak states are the most important causes of misery and poverty in the world.

Because most enterprise businesses in developing societies are either fully or partially owned and run by their governments, their style of business administration is not very much different from that of the government. To a great extent, the private sector in developing markets follows the same norm. People at the top of these organizations are appointed based on their ties and loyalty to the ruler or the governing inner circle. Similarly, directors appointed at the top of most of the private businesses are usually chosen based on their relationship to the owner. In both cases, the business or technical qualifications of those at the top have little to do with the selection process.

That said, it should be noted that there are some companies in these markets that are led by professionals, but they are exceptions. The norm is that the government and the loyal elite control and run the economy.

One might be tempted to think that since the minority controls the economy, the majority could prevail by democratic or otherwise (and possibly violent) means. But it is important to remember that the global marketplace protects these regimes.

"When a poor democratic majority collides with the market-dominant minority, the majority does not always prevail. Instead of a backlash against the market, there is a backlash against democracy. Often this antidemocracy backlash takes the

form of 'crony capitalism': corrupt, symbiotic alliances between indigenous leaders and the market-dominant minority. For the global marketplace, this is a cozy solution. The indigenous regime protects the market-dominant minority's wealth and businesses. In turn the World Bank and IMF supply loans." (Chua, 2003, p. 147)

Due to their monopolistic control of financial and legislative organizations, governing bodies and business owners who generally accumulated their wealth through their relationship with the governing body, merchandizing, real estate development, or similar traditional industries, have always been on the forefront of seizing the new opportunities provided by the market. The dilemma is that most of these people suddenly find themselves facing challenges imposed by globalization and an array of new industries that they wish to run the same way they have always run their traditional businesses. In the globalization era, where the information industry represents more than half the gross national product of modern industrial states, running modern knowledge-intensive businesses grounded in information technology, telecommunications, insurance, and financial investment certainly requires much more talent than loyalty.

Accustomed to managing the use of equipment and directing generally unskilled labor but lacking the qualifications and prerequisites to manage talented human capital, these loyal directors have been creating poor copies of similar businesses found in the West. Soroush, in *Reason, Freedom, and Democracy in Islam* (2000), describing the outcome of this situation, states that

> *"the result is the creation of half-industrial/ half-traditional hybrid systems that are incapable of managing their own affairs in the cultural, political, and world-historical arenas. For this reason it is better to keep the issue of development as a preoccupation of the elites rather than allowing it to turn into a chain fettering the movements of the masses,"* (p. 41)

Equipped with all the power and authority that would make the workers do what they want them to do, business directors in the developing markets never realized the need for the business leadership concept. Why would they need to influence an employee who would, in any event, happily or otherwise forcefully follow orders?

The other side of the problem is that the employees themselves, as indicated earlier, are not familiar with and most often do not ask for a more democratic environment. Similar to the grander society, any democratic extension introduced into the business environment would most certainly be abused and would cause more damage than good.

Contemporary talent-intensive industries newly introduced into developing markets cannot function with the same mentality that ran their traditional, muscle-oriented businesses. The challenge, then, is to discover how change and development can be effectively integrated into the business environments of developing markets.

Indeed, as Soroush suggests, the issue of development should be the preoccupation of the "elite," the educated, knowledgeable, and skilled people who constitute a very thin segment of today's business environment in developing markets. However, when hiring practices do not depend on technical qualifications, the true elite—those who could effect change—do not usually arrive at the top and are mostly found in the middle of an organization's hierarchy. Without the prerequisite of formal authority required to bring about change, these people find it hard to drive change and development in totally authoritative environments. How can they sell their ideas to the dictators at the top? How could they make the dictators do the right thing? How could they lead from the middle?

Although most of this book has been dedicated to describing the inapplicability of the concept of business leadership in developing markets, the middle of the developing societies and their business organizations are the areas where the leadership concept is most applicable. In this case, however, the leadership concept is essentially focused on influencing superiors and others at the top of the organization; quite the opposite of the usual downward application.

Although it has been argued that leadership is a concept of influence without authority, its application in modern organizations has usually been coupled with formal authority. Richard Shell and Mario Moussa, in their book *The Art of Woo: Using Strategic Persuasion to Sell Your Ideas* (2007, p. 22), state that

> *"even in an era of flat organizations and collaborative teamwork, formal authority serves as the basis for more influence moves at work than any other influence foundation."*

Lacking the formal authority, the elite in the developing societies must learn the skill that would enable them to influence those in the top and lead from the middle. The authors suggest six channels of persuasion: *1. Interest-based Persuasion, 2. Authority, 3. Politics, 4. Rationality, 5. Inspiration and Emotion – The Vision Channel, and 6. Relationships.* Other channels of persuasion, such as begging, shoe-shining and buttering up are also among the tactics that some individuals might use, but this book is about ethical methods and decent individual behavior.

As mentioned earlier, leading upward does not involve authority, leaving us with five other channels. All these channels would be worthless, however, if those on the top do not see a value in return for their cooperation (or "support," as they would prefer to call it). My experience tells me that education and, more importantly, giving credit for a job well done are the best reward to be given in exchange for their support.

Jim Collins, in his book *Good to Great* (2001), describes how level 5 leaders give away credit but assume responsibility at the same time.

> *"Level 5 leaders look out the window to apportion credit to factors outside themselves when things go well (and if they cannot find a specific person or event to give credit to, they credit good luck). At the same time, they look in the mirror to apportion responsibility, never blaming bad luck when things go poorly."* (p. 35)

Thus, those who wish to lead from the middle should not worry about the short-term credit but focus instead on the long-term development of the society. As Jeffrey J. Fox puts it in his book *How to Become CEO* (1998), "Be a credit maker, not a credit taker."

Leading from the Middle

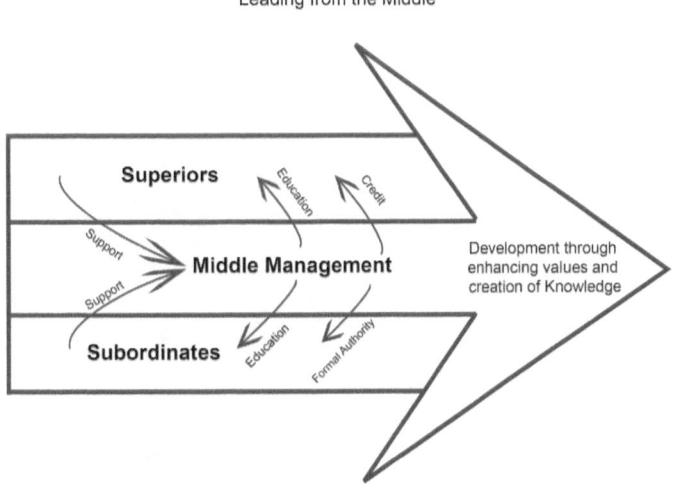

First, man hungers for bread.
As food is life's main thread.
When at long last he reaches satiety,
He seeks fame, the praise of poets and
notoriety.

Rumi

THE FUTURE: EVOLUTION NOT REVOLUTION

It is a well-known fact that knowledge, or at least the foundation of modern knowledge, originated in the East. The Mesopotamians, Egyptians, Persians, Indians, and Chinese each made their own great contribution to the creation of early human knowledge. The initial laws of human governance and social order, early knowledge of mathematics, development of the alphabet and writing, and religion are among many other significant products of what is often called the cradle of civilization. Up until the birth of the Greek philosopher Thales around 600 BC, these civilizations enjoyed cultural and economic superiority over neighboring less-developed societies.

Trading and commercial exchange between the East and the Greeks facilitated the transfer of knowledge to the West. It is argued that the Greek constructive criticism of otherwise sacred eastern knowledge sparked the first human "knowledge explosion" as described by Charles Van Doren in his book *A History of Knowledge* (1991). The reasons behind this knowledge explosion are beyond the scope of this book, but it was around that time that the Greeks began to take over the knowledge creation affair.

By about 350 BC, at the time of Alexander the Great's invasion of the East, while there was intellectual regression in the eastern nations, the Greeks, and then the Romans, built the greatest empires in human history with mathematics, philosophy, politics, and law as their primary intellectual products. By the mid-fifth century AD, the Roman Empire had collapsed and its fragmented nation-states were plunged into the Dark Ages. During this period, which lasted for more than 600 years, western cultural, intellectual, and economic conditions declined dramatically. Of all the intellectual disciplines, theology alone developed.

Two centuries later, in the mid-seventh century, Muslims were about to build their great empire in the East. Knowledge was once again centered in the East. Polymaths such as Avicenna, Averroes, Omar Khayyam, Nasir al-Din Tusi, Alpharabius, and Algorismi are only a few of those who contributed to building an Islamic golden age that lasted for more than 600 years. The 13th century marked the beginning of the decline of the number of Islamic scientists and Islamic science in general.

Once again, the science and knowledge of the East was taken up in the West to signal a new era of advancement: the Renaissance.

From the beginning of Renaissance in the 14th century until the modern era, Europe, later joined by the United States, has been the leader in the transmission of knowledge and in science and technology, whereas the rest of the world has become mere consumers of knowledge.

History of Knowledge

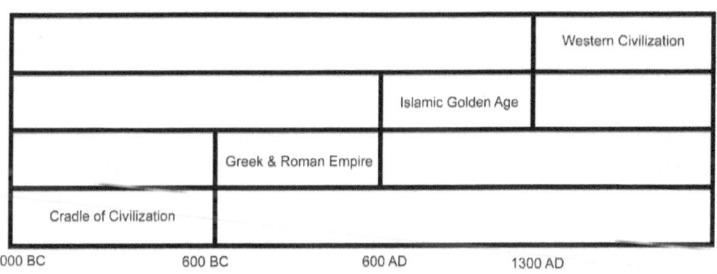

			Western Civilization
		Islamic Golden Age	
	Greek & Roman Empire		
Cradle of Civilization			

5000 BC   600 BC   600 AD   1300 AD

One very important lesson to be learned from this very brief history of knowledge is that the accrual of knowledge and cultural, social, and economic development are gradual processes. They need time to evolve and cannot be imposed or realized overnight. Those who wish to lead and bring sustainable growth need to consider this fact carefully. History has taught us that revolutionary and overnight changes may survive for a while but can never last for long. Communism is a great example of how a forceful, sudden cultural change brings quick material results—and always at a high cost in human dignity—but cannot survive for long.

With education as their primary preoccupation, leaders in the developing markets should not seek—nor expect—immediate results. They should be aware that developing markets simply lack the prerequisites. And although their role is to bring about change, they should be cautious in attempting to solve their unique problems using off-the-shelf solutions imported from the West. Leaders should be aware that thoughtless implementation of changes mandated by globalization (or what I call the western economic aggression) will most likely have ugly long-term consequences. Capitalism is a product of western civilization and, as Karl Marx predicted, it tends to widen the gap between the rich minority and the poor majority. Global capitalism is simply an exportation of this idea, which seeks to create a global capitalist society in which the gap exists between the West and the rest.

Leaders should be aware that revolutionary changes mandated by globalization with promises of prosperity and development will only lead to disasters in the long term. This is not to suggest that leaders in developing countries should not learn from the West; on the contrary, transferring western knowledge should be one of their priorities. But western knowledge should not be transferred for mere wholesale consumption; it should be employed as a basis for the development of local knowledge. And leaders also need to distinguish between knowledge and skills. Knowledge is the ability to solve problems but a skill is merely an application of knowledge. What is often transferred from the West to the developing countries is skill, not knowledge.

Leaders should start with education at the value level to enhance behavior. Enhanced behavior produces knowledge through problem-solving, and at that point, skills can be developed.

Levels of Education

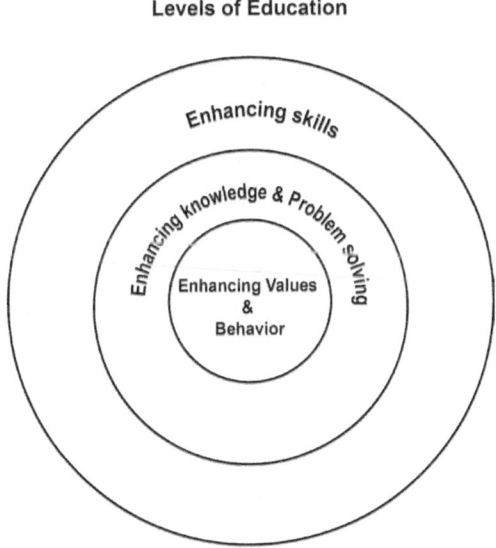

The dilemma is this: to initiate education at the value level, an acceptable level of social welfare is necessary. When people are busy all day trying to make ends meet, moving up to the value level is certainly not their first priority.

"The distress of acquiring one's daily bread, shelter, and clothing would hardly allow for engagement in arts and the pursuit of worldly knowledge and mystical gnosis." (Soroush, 2000, p. 44)

In the mostly poor developing markets, educating people at the value level is an impossible mission. To begin the long journey toward education and its benefits, leaders must first find ways to enhance the welfare of society.

A United Nations report titled "Globalization of R&D and Developing Countries" (2005) estimates that developing countries undertake less than eight percent of formal research and development activities globally and that much of their R&D is through public, state-supported organizations. The same report affirms that many developing countries have fared only moderately in growth, knowledge, and welfare creation because their R&D efforts have remained underfunded and disconnected from the private sector. Consequently, one could argue that in order to bring growth and development to developing markets, the private sector should play a more active role in the process of knowledge creation.

Much of the failure of the public sector in this regard can be attributed to its inability to commercialize innovation. If knowledge and innovation do not translate into economic value, they are considered a waste of money. This would certainly keep the R&D expenditure at its current levels in the developing markets as it represents cost rather than investment. Commercialization of innovation through increased investment in R&D in the private sector could positively enhance the creation of wealth and job opportunities and consequently the welfare of the society.

This would take time, but the simple importation of quick fixes will always keep markets developing but never developed.

Leaders should be aware that in order to develop, they need to be able to solve their unique problems through their own thinking and experience. Knowledge is the ability to solve problems; if they keep on having their problems solved for them, they will never develop knowledge! They will learn, of course, but they will never contribute to knowledge development, creation of wealth, and social development.

It cannot be emphasized enough that the issue of development is a gradual process: it takes time.

Those who have a genuine desire to bring about change, sustainable growth, and knowledge development should be cautious about bringing in overnight change that accords with western mandates. Refusing to be poor copies of the West, they should strive to maintain their own unique identity and their own share of positive contributions to human and knowledge development.

Soros (2002), commenting on development projects imported to the developing markets and implemented by foreign experts, argues that most of these programs do not succeed because of the lack of ownership by the locals. He states that

> "when the experts leave, not much remains. Programs that are imported rather than home grown often do not take root." (p. 23)

Leaders also ought not be tempted to measure their achievements using the contemporary market definition of success. Today, success is primarily measured by materialistic means—how much money one can accumulate or what degree of social status one can achieve. Defining success using these criteria will force leaders into expecting immediate results and consequently lead them to adopt quick fixes.

On the subject of success, Covey (1990, p. 18) says

> "I began to feel more and more that much of the success literature of the past 50 years was superficial. It was filled with social image consciousness, techniques and quick fixes with social band-aids and aspirin that addressed acute problems and sometimes even appeared to solve them temporarily, but left the underlying chronic problems untouched to fester and resurface time and again."

Unfortunately, with the ever-increasing pressure on today's developing societies and their businesses to achieve results in the short term, sustainable growth is dismissed. And adopting quick fixes, where ends justify the means regardless of the long-term consequences, is not only tolerated but sometimes even rewarded, and those involved are considered to be highly successful leaders.

Leaders should redefine success and measure it first by its level of positive contribution to humanity. Only then will they be sure that they are on the right path to development.

REDEFINING SUCCESS

How would you describe a successful person?

I don't want to be too subjective, but I am confident that if this question is asked in a survey, most answers would not go beyond describing personal earthly and materialistic achievements. It is unfortunate that the unit of measurement for success has become money-centered and worldly, wherein the bottom line is, the amount of money you have defines how successful you are.

Positive contributions to humanity and society—being a good son, a good mother, a God-fearing man, having a thirst for knowledge and enlightenment—these might entitle you to seize the title of "good" but they are not enough for you to be considered "successful."

Did today's criteria for success apply a hundred years ago? Five hundred years ago? I don't think so. Why have we adopted money as the ultimate criteria for success?

My guess is that man has moved into a smaller world, in many ways a world that does not go beyond materiality. Earlier, man lived in a bigger world. Materiality was part, but not all of it. Thus, success was defined in broader terms—terms that could embrace metaphysical elements and non-tangible goals. In the bigger world, man's life on earth was a brief journey and the ultimate objective was to prepare for the real life. For this reason, man's success depended on and was defined by how ready he was for the next life. Ethical behavior, or being good, was the preferred criteria for success.

In today's smaller, materialistic world, real life is the life we live today. Man might admit to believing in the next life, but his actions speak louder than his words. In a small world that is not part of a bigger picture and lacks any metaphysical extensions, we have no choice but to choose materialistic criteria to define our success.

But I am frightened by this picture. Because material resources are limited, not all of us can be "successful." Striving for success would eventually lead to conflicts. Also, in a small world man looks somewhat bigger than he does in a big world—and feeling big is dangerous; it leads to arrogance and vanity. We should always remember that Satan was kicked out of heaven because of his arrogance.

This is not an invitation for poverty; it is an attempt to redefine success.

Let's be successful!

Nay! Verily, man does transgress all bounds (in disbelief and evil deeds) …
Because he considers himself self-sufficient, surely!
Unto your Lord is the return.
The Quran, The Clot 6,7,8

I would never die for my beliefs because I might be wrong.

Bertrand Russell

BIBLIOGRAPHY

Robert F. Bruner et al., *The Portable MBA*. 4th ed. Hoboken, N.J.: John Wiley and Sons, 2003.

Amy Chua, *World on Fire: How Exporting Free Market Democracy Breeds Ethnic Hatred and Global Instability*. London: Arrow Books, 2003.

James G. Clawson, *A Leader's Guide to Why People Behave the Way They Do*. Charlottesville: University of Virginia Darden School Foundation, 2001.

Allan R. Cohen and David Bradford, *Influence Without Authority*. 2nd ed. Hoboken, N.J.: John Wiley and Sons, 2005.

Jim Collins, *Good to Great*. New York: HarperCollins, 2001.

Stephen R. Covey, *The 7 Habits of Highly Effective People*. New York: Simon & Schuster, 1990.

Hernando de Soto, *The Mystery of Capital*, New York: Basic Books, 2000.

Charles Van Doren, *A History of Knowledge*. New York: Random House, 1991.

Peter F. Drucker, "Managing Oneself." *Harvard Business Review* (March–April 1999): 65–74.

Jeffrey Fox, *How to Become a CEO: The Rules for Rising to the Top of any Organization*. New York: Hyperion, 1998.

Sigmund Freud, *The Ego and the Id*. London: The Hogarth Press, 1949.

Daniel Goleman, "Leadership that Gets Results." *Harvard Business Review* (March–April 2000).

"Influence: Your Mechanism for Using Power." From the series *Harvard Business Essentials*. [Boston: Harvard Business Publishing].

Micheline Ishay, *The History of Human Rights*. Berkeley: University of California Press, 2003.

Robert Kreitner, *Management*. Boston: Houghton Mifflin, 1995.

Vijay Mahajan and Kamini Banga, *The 86% Solution*. Upper Saddle River, N.J.: Pearson Education Inc., 2006.

Abraham Maslow, *Motivation and Personality*. New York: Harper and Row, 1954.

Douglas McGregor, *The Human Side of Enterprise*. New York: McGraw-Hill, 1960.

Michael Nicholson, *Mahatma Gandhi, Leader of Indian Independence*. Farmington Hills, Mich.: Blackbirch Press, 2003.

Benjamin Pogrund, *Nelson Mandela, Leader Against Apartheid*. Farmington Hills, Mich.: Blackbirch Press, 2003.

Karl Popper, *The Open Society and Its Enemies*. London: Routledge, 1945.

Stephen Robbins, *Organizational Behavior*. Upper Saddle River, N.J.: Pearson Education Inc., 2005.

G. Richard Shell and Mario Moussa, *The Art of Woo: Using Strategic Persuasion to Sell Your Ideas*. New York: Penguin Group, 2007.

George Soros, *George Soros on Globalization*. New York: PublicAffairs, 2002.

Abdolkarim Soroush, *Reason, Freedom and De-mocracy in Islam*. New York: Oxford University Press, 2000.

United Nations report, "Globalization of R&D and Developing Countries," Geneva, 2005.

Jack Welch and Suzy Welch, *Winning*. New York: HarperCollins, 2005.